BLAZERS

SUPER SPEED

DIRT BIKE Racing

BY LORI POLYDOROS

Reading Consultant:
Barbara J. Fox
Professor Emerita
North Carolina State University

CAPSTONE PRESS
a capstone imprint

Blazers Books are published by Capstone Press,
1710 Roe Crest Drive, North Mankato, Minnesota 56003
www.capstonepub.com

Library of Congress Cataloging-in-Publication Data
Polydoros, Lori, 1968–
  Dirt bike racing / by Lori Polydoros.
      pages cm.—(Blazers. Super speed.)
  Includes bibliographical references and index.
  Summary: "Describes dirt bikes and dirt bike racing, including safety features and rules governing dirt bike racing"—Provided by publisher.
  ISBN 978-1-4765-0120-8 (library binding)
  ISBN 978-1-4765-3368-1 (ebook PDF)
1. Motorcycle racing—Juvenile literature. 2. Trail bikes—Juvenile literature. I. Title.
  GV1060.P637 2014
  796.7'5—dc23   2013003670

Editorial Credits
Gene Bentdahl, designer; Jennifer Walker, production specialist

Photo Credits
Alamy: CTK/Rene Fluger, 20-21 (both), Findlay, 25, The Photolibrary Wales/Andrew Orchard, 19; Andy Kawa Photography, 22-23; Dreamstime: Anthony Aneese Totah Jr, 8-9; Newscom: Cal Sport Media/Mat Gdowski, 14-15, imago sportfotodienst, cover; Shutterstock: B.Stefanov, 5, i4lcocl2, 10-11, Lukich, 19, Natursports, 26, PhotoStock10, 7, TachePhoto, 12, 13, taelove7, 16-17, Ventura, 29

Artistic Effects
Shutterstock: 1xpert, My Portfolio, rodho

Capstone Press thanks Peter terHorst for sharing his motorcycling expertise during the production of this book.

Printed in the United States of America in Stevens Point, Wisconsin.
032013   007227WZF13

TABLE OF CONTENTS

READY TO RACE

Dirt bike racers speed over rough ground, bumpy tracks, and even ice. In some races they splash through mud or ride over telephone poles lying on the ground. Winning takes more than a fast bike. It takes skill and bravery.

FAST FACT

The American Motorcyclist Association (AMA) has been holding motorcycle competitions since 1924.

Dirt bikes are built to handle high jumps and sharp turns. Made to be lightweight, a dirt bike changes direction easily. Strong **suspensions** help riders tackle bumps and jumps. Knobby tires help grip loose dirt.

suspension—the system that helps smooth out the up and down movements as a vehicle goes over bumps

FAST FACT

In a triple jump, riders launch over three jumps at once. Most Supercross racers can jump at least 70 feet (21 meters).

Supercross racing takes place on dirt tracks in huge **stadiums**. Riders compete in **qualifiers** for a chance to race in the main event.

stadium—a large, usually roofless building with rows of seats for fans

qualifier—a race to decide who can advance to the next level of competition

Motocross is one of the oldest types of motorcycle racing. Motocross racers speed around outdoor tracks. Racers compete in two **motos** in each **class**.

moto—a single motocross race; each motocross event includes two motos

class—a competitive group with similar skill levels and machines

Enduro racing is not just a test of speed. Enduro racers stop at **checkpoints** and ride to the finish line within certain time limits. They twist through forests and across deserts. The tricky routes include **obstacles** such as water and logs.

checkpoint—a location in a race where the arrival time of each rider is recorded

obstacle—something that gets in the way; obstacles on enduro courses include logs and rocks

Endurocross combines Supercross courses with enduro obstacles. Riders compete on narrow stadium courses. They race over logs and splash through deep water.

PHOTO DIAGRAM

1. REAR FENDER
2. EXHAUST PIPE
3. ENGINE
4. FRONT FENDER
5. FRONT SUSPENSION
6. FRAME
7. ENGINE GUARD
8. KNOBBY TIRES

16

3

4

5

6

7

TOUGH TRACKS AND TASKS

Flat track races were the first type of organized motorcycle races held in the United States. Racers zip around dirt tracks shaped like ovals or figure eights. Riders race on **modified** bikes made to suit each type of track.

modified—changed in some way

SPEEDWAY RACING

FAST FACT

Speedway racing is another popular dirt track event. The bikes have no brakes or gears. Riders slide sideways around bends to keep up their speed.

SPIKED
TIRES

Ice racing takes place on oval courses. Bikes need spiked tires to grip the ice. Riders race at speeds up to 80 miles (130 km) per hour. They lean so far into the curves that the handlebars touch the ice!

Riders dash up steep hills in hill climbing events. The rider who reaches the top in the shortest time wins. If nobody reaches the top, the rider who went the farthest and quickest wins.

Hare scrambles usually take place in **rugged** areas. Riders race to the finish line on long, looped courses. They face obstacles such as mud and water.

FAST FACT

Races in the AMA National Hare Scrambles series last two hours. The tracks are loops of 8 to 15 miles (13 to 24 km).

rugged—rough and uneven

Racetracks for trial competitions include **vertical** climbs and steep **descents**. Racers ride slowly around rocks and logs. They lose points if their feet touch the ground.

vertical—straight up and down

descent—a move from a higher place to a lower place

SKILLS AND THRILLS

Dirt bike racers speed up steep hills and slide into tight turns. These extreme athletes have talent and a taste for adventure that keep fans coming back for more.

GLOSSARY

checkpoint (CHEK-point)—a location in a race where the arrival time of each rider is recorded

class (CLASS)—a competitive group with similar skill levels and machines

descent (dee-SENT)—a move from a higher place to a lower place

modified (MOD-uh-fyed)—changed in some way

moto (MOH-toh)—a single motocross race; each motocross event includes two motos

obstacle (OB-stuh-kuhl)—something that gets in the way; obstacles on enduro courses include logs and rocks

qualifier (KWAHL-uh-fye-uhr)—a race to decide who can advance to the next level of competition

rugged (RUHG-id)—rough and uneven

stadium (STAY-dee-uhm)—a large, usually roofless building with rows of seats for fans

suspension (suh-SPEN-shuhn)—the system that helps smooth out the up and down movements as a vehicle goes over bumps

vertical (VUR-tuh-kuhl)—straight up and down

READ MORE

Aloian, Molly. *Motorcycles.* Vehicles on the Move. New York: Crabtree, 2011.

Doeden, Matt. *Supercross.* Dirt Bike World. Mankato, Minn.: Capstone Press, 2011.

Holter, James. *Dirt Bike Racers.* Kid Racers. Berkeley Heights, N.J.: Enslow Publishers, 2010.

INTERNET SITES

FactHound offers a safe, fun way to find Internet sites related to this book. All of the sites on FactHound have been researched by our staff.

Here's all you do:

Visit *www.facthound.com*

Type in this code: 9781476501208

Check out projects, games and lots more at
www.capstonekids.com

INDEX